CL

SLANG

A POCKET GUIDE TO
CANADIAN
WORDS & PHRASES

So you don't look stupid
when trying to understand
Canadian language

PREFACE

For those who have never been to Canada, hearing people talk can sound like a foreign language. A unique vocabulary has been developed which can be utterly mystifying to outsiders. This mini illustrated 'dictionary' of Canadian words and sayings is here to rescue you.

EH!

6IX

The six former cities that now make up Toronto. The area code 416.

B'Y

A term derived from "boy" and is often used informally to refer to someone or address a friend.

BACHELOR APARTMENT

An apartment with a room containing a small kitchen, dining room, living room and bedroom. You can still have a big party in small spaces.

BEAKING

Used in Western Canada to describe making fun of someone.

BEAUTY

Used to describe something that was done very well. Wow! What a beauty!

BEAVER TAILS

A sweet Candian pastry treat.
They don't taste like beavers.

BIBITTE

Used mostly in Quebec, it is a Canadian French term for a bug or insect.

BIFFED

To fall or to trip up. It can also be used to describe when someone makes a mistake or messes something up.

BITTIE

An attractive woman.

BLUE NOSER

Anyone from Nova Scotia. The name comes from the Blue Nose ship.

BOOTER

Often used in Western Canada, it is when you step into snow or a puddle deep enough that water ends up into your boot to give you cold and wet socks.

BOOZE CAN

An illegal after-hours bar. Ghosts don't visit often as they don't like spirits.

BRITISH CALIFORNIA

British Columbia, the California of Canada. Known for its warmer winters and laidback lifestyle.

BUNNYHUG

A hoodie, used in the province of Saskatchewan.

BUTTER TART

Small pastry shells filled with butter, maple syrup, brown sugar and raisins.

BY TOWN

Ottowa. It is the second coldest national capital in the world after Ulaanbaatar, the capital of Mongolia.

CAESAR

A cocktail that is similar to a Bloody Mary but made with clamato juice.

CANADIAN TUXEDO

An informal outfit consisting of a blue denim jacket and blue jeans. Very stylish.

CANUCK

A Canadian. Also the nickname of the professional hockey team. Equivalent of "Brit" for someone from the United Kingdom.

CHAMPAGNE BIRTHDAY

When your age is the date of your birthday. For example when your birthday is on the 21st and you turn 21.

CHESTERFIELD

A term usually used by older people to refer to a couch.

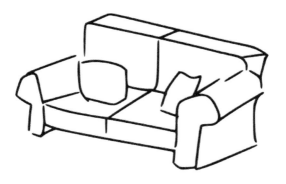

CHINOOK

A warm wind that blows over a mountain in winter which melts the snow and raises the temperature.

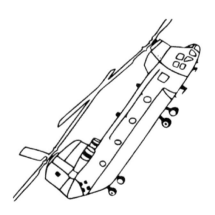

CHIRPING

Trash-talking the opposition during a competition. Also used to describe making fun of someone. It's all about having fun with words and humour.

CHUCKLEHEAD

Insult to describe someone as stupid. A playful way to point out someone's goofy antics.

CINQ À SEPT

Often heard in Montreal and translates to "5 to 7," it is the equivalent of happy hour. It's a very happy time.

CLAMATO JUICE

Clam and tomato juice used for a Caesar.

CLICK

A kilometre, the unit of distance. Also spelt Klick.

COWTOWN

The city of Calgary. Calgary is known for having one of the sunniest climates of all major cities in Canada.

DECKED OUT

Something that is decorated or someone who is dressed up. You can get decked out to go to a party and the party venue itself could be decked out with decorations.

DEP

A convenience store in the French-speaking Quebec. Short for dépanneur.

DINGED

When your wallet gets hit with an unexpected expense. Fined money.

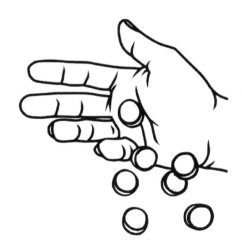

DOUBLE-DOUBLE

Regular coffee with two sugars and two creams.

DOUGHHEAD

A lighthearted insult mainly used in Ontario to describe someone as stupid or slow witted.

EH

A stereotypical interjection added to the end of a sentence to turn it into a question or to seek confirmation.

FILL YER BOOTS

Make yourself at home or make yourself comfortable.

FREEZIES

The sugary treat that comes frozen in a plastic tube.

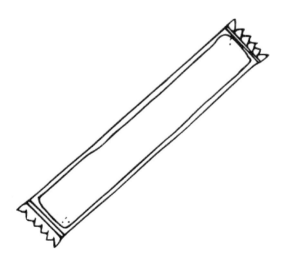

GARBURATOR

The garbage disposal that is usually installed under a kitchen sink.

GITCH

Underpants. You're almost guaranteed to get some gitch as a Christmas present. Also called gotch.

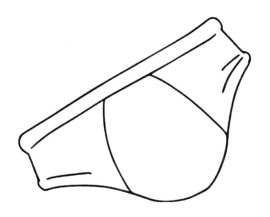

GIVE'ER

Go hard and give it your all.

GONG SHOW

A situation that is out of control. Often in a funny way.

GORBY

Mainly used in Ontario to describe loud and ignorant tourists.

GOTCH

Underpants. Also called gitch.

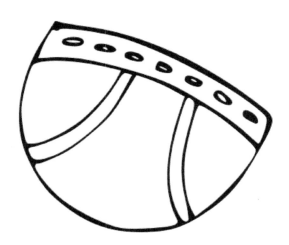

GTA

Greater Toronto Area which includes Toronto as well as neighbouring suburbs.

HALIFORNIA

Commonly shortened to Hali,
this is Halifax, Nova Scotia.

HALIGONIAN

Someone who is from the city of Halifax in Nova Scotia.

HANG A LARRY

Take a left turn.

HANG A ROGER

take a right turn.

HOMO MILK

Homogenized milk or whole milk with 3.25% fat.

HOOPED

The equivalent of 'screwed' to describe when you may be stuck in a difficult situation.

HYDRO

Electricity. Derived from the fact that electricity in Ontario is primarily generated by hydroelectric power plants.

HYDRO BILL

An electricity bill, the highlight of the month for nobody.

JAMBUSTER

A doughnut filled with jam.
One of life's simple pleasures.

JESUS MURPHY

An exclamation used to express surprise, frustration, or disbelief.

KEENER

Someone who works hard to try and please others (a brown noser).

KERFUFFLE

A commotion or fuss. A way of referring to a fight, argument or conflict. A great word that rolls off the tongue.

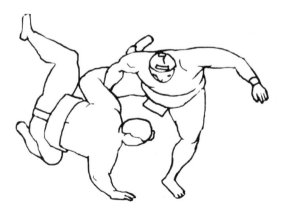

KETCHUP CHIPS

Ketchup flavoured potato chips.

KITTY-CORNER

Used to describe the location of a place that is diagonally across from a point.

KNAPSACK

A backpack or rucksack.

LINEUP

A line or queue of people waiting.

LOONIE

A one dollar coin. The name derived from a picture of the loon (a Canadian bird) on the coin.

LOONIE BIN

A store where you can find a wide variety of cheap things or second-hand items.

MAY 2-4 WEEKEND

May 24th (Victoria Day), Queen Victoria's birthday. A national holiday.

MICKEY

A small bottle of alcohol that can fit into a pocket.

MOLSON MUSCLE

A beer belly. An alternative way of acknowledging the potential consequences of indulging in beer consumption.

MOUNTIE

A member of The Royal
Canadian Mounted Police
(RCMP), the national police
service of Canada.

MUSKOKA CHAIR

Wooden chairs made for lounging that are usually brightly painted with a a low seat. They have a very high back and thick arms.

NANAIMO BAR

A dessert made of an almond and walnut base layered with vanilla butter icing and covered in a layer of melted chocolate.

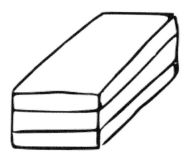

NEWFIE

Anyone from Newfoundland.
Newfoundland is known for
having its own time zone,
called Newfoundland Standard
Time (NST) which is 30 minutes
ahead of Atlantic Standard
Time (AST).

NIZE IT

Toronto slang for telling
someone to shut up.

OUT FOR A RIP

Head out for a drive.

PARKADE

A multi-story parking lot.

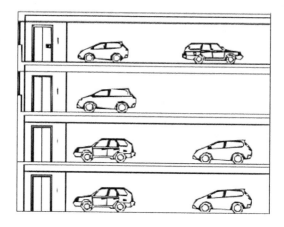

PARKETTE

A small park or small urban green spaces.

POGIE

On government welfare assistance.

POP

A carbonated drink.

POUTINE

French fries draped with cheese curds and gravy. Delicious.

REGULAR

A coffee with one cream and one sugar.

RINK RAT

A person who spends most of their time at the skating rink.

ROTTED

Feeling angry or disappointed.
Used in Eastern Canada.

RUNNERS

A pair of running shoes.

SCIVEY

A term used to describe someone who cannot be trusted or is sneaky. Watch out!

SHIT-KICKERS

A pair of shoes you don't mind getting covered in dirt and mud. You could kick shit with them if you wanted to.

SNOWBIRDS

Canadians who move to warmer climates in the winter to avoid the cold.

SOPHONSIFIED

Be be satisfied in reference to appetite. Sufficiently full.

STUBBLEJUMPER

Anyone from the Prairies. So called because when the fields are plowed, it looks like stubble.

TEXAS MICKEY

A large 3 litre bottle of alcohol. It is thought to have originated from the idea that everything is bigger in Texas.

THE PEG

The city of Winnipeg which is also known as the Gateway to the West.

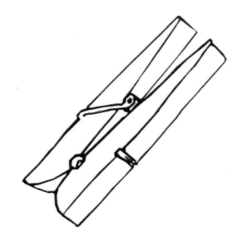

THE ROCK

A term used for Newfoundland.

TIMBITS

Delicious bite-sized doughnut holes made from leftover doughnut dough, fried in vegetable oil.

TIMS

The fast food chain Tim Hortons. Also called Timmies.

TOONIE

A two dollar coin.

TOQUE

A knitted hat worn in cold weather. It comes in handy in the northern parts of Canada.

TTC

Totonto Transit Commission – the agency that provides transit services to Torontonians so they can get around in style.

TWO-FOUR

A case of 24 beers.

X4

WASHROOM

The toilet.

WHALE'S TAIL

Another name for beaver tails.

YARN

To chat.

BEAUTY

BEAUTY

BEAUTY

BEAUTY

BEAUTY

BEAUTY

Printed in Great Britain
by Amazon